Easy To C

2 Hour Slippers

Volume 2: Summer Slippers

By

Vicki Becker

Copyright Information Page

Vicki Becker

www.vickisdesigns.com

First Printing, 2013

ISBN-13: 978-1490336350

ISBN-10: 1490336354

Printed in the United States of America

Contents

Introduction

These cute slippers are very quick and easy to make. The designs use cotton yarns for cool comfortable slippers. The pattern instructions are for 4 different styles of ladies slippers in three sizes. Patterns for three different embellishments are also included.

I hope you enjoy my pattern for these easy to crochet slippers.

General Instructions

Gauge

Gauge is determined by the tightness or looseness of your work and will affect the finished size of your project. Make a small section of the pattern before starting your project to check the gauge.

Understanding Symbols

As asterisk (*) indicates that the directions immediately following are to be repeated the given number of times in addition to the original.

Parenthesis is used to set off a group of instructions worked a number of times or in a particular stitch. For example, "(3 dc, ch 1, 3 dc) in each corner" or "(3 dc, ch 3) 3 times".

How to read patterns with multiple sizes

When crocheting or knitting a pattern with multiple sizes parentheses are often used to include additional information for other sizes. For example, if the instructions read chain 12 (14, 16), you would chain 12 for size small, 14 for medium, and 16 for large.

Motif Centers

After making a center ring I always crochet over the tail end of the yarn. I can then pull the end of the yarn to make a nice tight center.

Standard Yarn Weight System

Most yarn and thread now come with a weight number on the wrapper. I provide the weight number of the yarn or thread I used to design each pattern. This makes it much easier to make substitutions.

Helpful Hints

Changing Colors

To change color in single or double crochet you always work the last two loops on the hook off with the new color.

For single crochet, pull up a loop in the current color you are using, draw the new color through the last two loops on the hook to complete the single crochet stitch.

For double crochet, yarn over, pull up a loop in the current color you are using, draw through two loops, draw the new color through the last two loops on the hook to complete the double crochet stitch.

Size G Crochet Hook

Have you ever noticed that size G crochet hooks come in different millimeters? Depending on the manufacturer the size can be anywhere from 4.0mm to 4.5mm. The 4.5mm can also be called a size 7. If your gauge is just slightly off you may just need a different size G hook!

Make your slippers non-slip!

Knitted or crocheted slippers are very slippery on laminate, hard wood, or tile floors. There are several methods to make them non-slip.

I use Puffy Paint. You can find puffy paint just about anywhere that sells craft supplies. Just dot some on the slipper bottom or make some squiggly lines or swirls.

Available on-line is Regia ABS Latex or Efco Sock Stop.

Abbreviations

Abbreviations			
beg	beginning	rep (s)	repeat (s)
ch (s)	chain (s)	rnd (s)	round (s)
dc	double crochet	sc	single crochet
dtr	double treble crochet	sk	skip
hdc	half double crochet	sl st	slip stitch
lp (s)	loop (s)	sp (s)	space (s)
pat	pattern	st (s)	stitch (es)
rem	remaining	tr	treble crochet
yo	yarn over		
MC	main color	CC	contrasting color

Crochet Terms

British vs American English Crochet Terms			
British English		**US - American English**	
Double Crochet	dc	Single Crochet	sc
Half Treble	htr	Half Double Crochet	hdc
Treble	tr	Double Crochet	dc
Double Treble	dtr	Treble	tr
Triple Treble	trtr	Double Treble	dtr
Miss		Skip	
Tension		Gauge	
Yarn Over Hook	yoh	Yarn Over	yo
All pattern instructions use US terms.			

Granny Ballet Flats

Instructions

Size: Small (5-6) Medium (7-8) Large (9-10)

Materials: Lily's Sugar'n Cream or any number 4 cotton yarn.

Main Color: 2 ounces (56.7g)

Contrasting Color and Flowers: 1 ounce (28.4g) color of your choice.

Two 1-inch buttons (optional)

Tapestry or yarn needle

Hook: Size H (5.0mm) crochet hook or size to obtain gauge

Gauge: 4 dc = 1 inch 2 rows = 1 inch

Note: Numbers in parenthesis are for medium and large sizes.

With MC ch 4, join with a sl st to form a ring.

Rnd 1: Ch 3. 11 dc in ring. Join with a sl st to top of first ch 3.

Rnd 2: Ch 3. 1 dc in same sp as last sl st. * 2 dc in next st, rep from * around. Join with a sl st to top of first ch 3. 24 dc.

Rnd 3: *For small size only.* Ch 3. 1 dc in same sp as last sl st. 1 dc in each of next 7 sts. *2 dc in next st. 1 dc in each of next 7 sts. Rep from * around. Join with a sl st to top of first ch 3. 27 dc.

Rnd 3: *For medium and large sizes.* Ch 3. 1 dc in same sp as last sl st. 1 dc in each of next 3 sts. *2 dc in next st. 1 dc in each of next 3 sts. Rep from * around. Join with a sl st to top of first ch 3. 30 dc.

Rnd 4: Ch 3. 2 dc in same sp as last sl st. *Sk 2 dc, 3 dc in next st. Rep from * around. Join with a sl st to top of first ch 3. 9 (10, 10) shells.

Rnd 5: Ch 3. *3 dc in sp between next 2 shells. Rep from * around to last sp. 2 dc in last sp. Join with a sl st to top of first ch 3. 9 (10, 10) shells.

Rnd 6: Ch 3. 2 dc in first sp. *3 dc in sp between next 2 shells. Rep from * around. Join with a sl st to top of first ch 3. 9 (10, 10) shells.

Rnd 7: Ch 3. *3 dc in sp between next 2 shells. Rep from * around to last sp. 2 dc in last sp. Join with a sl st to top of first ch 3. 9 (10, 10) shells. Ch 3. Turn.

Note: You will now be working in rows for all sizes. Medium and Large instructions are in parenthesis.

Row 1: 1 dc in first sp. 3 dc in each of next 5 (6,6) sps. 2 dc in next sp. Ch 3. Turn.

Row 2: 3 dc in first sp. 3 dc in each of next 5 (6, 6) sps. Dc in top of ch 3 of previous row. Ch 3. Turn.

Row 3: Dc in same sp as turning ch. 3 dc in next 5 (6, 6) sps. 2 dc in top of ch 3. Ch 3. Turn.

Rep rows 2-3, 3 (4, 5) more times.

Fasten off leaving a length of yarn to sew center back of slipper. With yarn end threaded in tapestry needle sew slipper heel together.

Edging: *(main color or a contrasting color)*

Rnd 1: Rejoin yarn with sc around bar of dc just to the left of heel. Sc around same bar. Sc evenly around top edge of slipper. Join with a sl st to first sc. Fasten off.

Flowers (make 2): With CC, ch 23.

Row 1: Sc in 5th ch from hk (counts as beg ch 2 sp). *Ch 2, sk 1 ch, sc in next ch. Rep from * across row. 10 ch 2 sps. Ch 1. Turn.

Row 2: Sc, ch 1, 3 dc, ch 1, sc in each ch 2 sp across row. 10 flower petals. Fasten off leaving a long tail of yarn for sewing flower. Twist flower petals into a pleasing shape and sew securely in place. Sew just off center of each slipper. Refer to photo of slipper for placement of flowers.

Optional Two Layer Flower

Bottom Layer: Ch 4, join with a sl st to form a ring.

Rnd 1: Ch 3. 11 dc in ring. Join with a sl st to top of first ch 3.

Rnd 2: Ch 3. *Sc in next st, ch 3. Rep from * around. Join with a sl st in bottom of first ch 3. Fasten off. Leave long tail of yarn for sewing to slipper.

Top Layer: Ch 4, join with a sl st to form a ring.

Rnd 1: Ch 3. Dc, ch 3, sc in ring. *Ch 3, dc, ch 3, sc in ring 4 times more. Fasten off. Leave long tail of yarn to sew layers together. 5 petals.

Finishing: Sew top layer to the bottom layer. Attach a button to the top layer and then sew flower to slipper using long tail of yarn from the bottom layer.

Two Tone Ballet Flats

Instructions

Size: Small (5-6) Medium (7-8) Large (9-10)

Materials: Lily's Sugar'n Cream or any number 4 cotton yarn.

Main Color: 2 ounces (56.7g)

Contrasting Color: 1 ounce (28.4g)

Tapestry or yarn needle

Hook: Size H (5.0mm) crochet hook or size to obtain gauge

Gauge: 4 dc = 1 inch 2 rows = 1 inch

Note: Numbers in parenthesis are for medium and large sizes.

With CC, Ch 4. Join with a sl st to form a ring.

Rnd 1: Ch 3. 11 dc in ring. Join with a sl st to top of first ch 3.

Rnd 2: Ch 3. 1 dc in same sp as last sl st. * 2 dc in next st, rep from * around. Join with a sl st to top of first ch 3. 24 dc.

Rnd 3: *For small size only.* Ch 3. 1 dc in same sp as last sl st. 1 dc in each of next 7 sts. *2 dc in next st. 1 dc in each of next 7 sts. Rep from * around. Join with a sl st to top of first ch 3. 27 dc.

Rnd 3: *For medium and large sizes.* Ch 3. 1 dc in same sp as last sl st. 1 dc in each of next 3 sts. *2 dc in next st. 1 dc in each of next 3 sts. Rep from * around. Join with a sl st to top of first ch 3. 30 dc.

Rnd 4: *For small size only.* Ch 3. 1 dc in each st around. Join with a sl st to top of first ch 3. 27 dc.

Rnd 4: *For sizes medium and large.* Ch 3. 1 dc in each st around. Join with a sl st to top of first ch 3. 30 dc.

Rnd 5: *For all sizes.* Ch 4 (counts as 1 dc, ch 1). Dc in same sp (V-st made). *Sk 2 dc, dc, ch 1, dc in next st (V-st made). Rep from * around. Join with a sl st to ch 3 of beg ch 4. 9 (10, 10) V-sts.

Rnd 6: Sl st in ch 1 sp of first V-st. Ch 4. Dc in same sp. *V-st in ch 1 sp of each V-st around. Join with a sl st in ch 3 of beg ch 4. 9 (10, 10) V-sts.

Rnd 7: Attach MC in same sp as sl st. Ch 3. Dc in each dc and ch sp around. 27 (30, 30) dc.

Note: You will now be working in rows for all sizes. Medium and Large instructions are in parenthesis.

Row 1: Ch 3 (counts as 1st dc). 1 dc in each of next 20 (22, 22) sts. Ch 3. Turn. 21 (23, 23) dc.

Rows 2-9 (10, 12): 1 dc in each st across. Ch 3. Turn. 21 (23, 23) dc.

Row 10 (11, 13): 1 dc in each of next 9 (10, 10) sts. Work next 3 sts together as follows: (yo, insert hook in next st, draw up lp, yo, draw through 2 lps) 3 times, yo, draw through 4 lps on hook. 1 dc in each of next 9 (10, 10) sts. Fasten off leaving a length of yarn to sew center back of slipper. With yarn end threaded in tapestry needle sew slipper heel together.

Edging

Rnd 1: Rejoin yarn with sc around bar of dc just to the left of heel. Sc around same bar. 2 sc around each bar and 1 sc in each st across toe. Join with a sl st to first sc. Fasten off.

Drawstring (optional): Ch 90. Fasten off. Starting at heel weave through the top edge of slipper just under edging and through the shells across the toe.

Flowers (optional): Ch 23.

Row 1: Sc in 5th ch from hk (counts as beg ch 2 sp). *Ch 2, sk 1 ch, sc in next ch. Rep from * across row. 10 ch 2 sps. Ch 1. Turn.

Row 2: Sc, ch 1, 3 dc, ch 1, sc in each ch 2 sp across row. 10 flower petals. Fasten off leaving a long tail of yarn for sewing flower. Twist flower petals into a pleasing shape and sew securely in place. Sew just off center of each slipper. Refer to photo of slipper for placement of flowers.

Granny Square Slippers

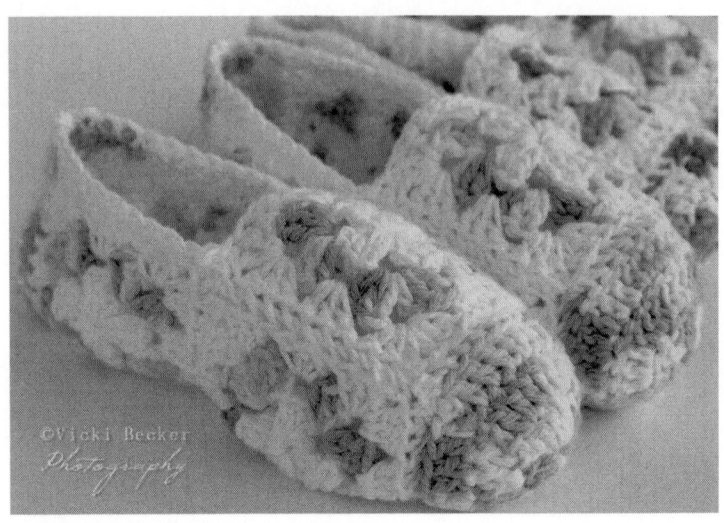

Instructions

Size: Small (5-6) Medium (7-8) Large (9-10)

Materials: Lily's Sugar'n Cream or any number 4 cotton yarn.

Main Color: 2 ounces (56.7g)

Contrasting Color: 1 ounce (28.4g)

Tapestry or yarn needle

Hook: Sizes G (4.25mm) and H (5.0mm) crochet hook or size to obtain gauge

Gauge: 4 dc = 1 inch 2 rows = 1 inch

Granny Squares: Small = 3" Medium-Large = 3 1/4"

Granny Squares (Make 10)

The 3 sizes are made by using different size crochet hooks.

Small: G (4.25mm) or size to obtain gauge. 3" square

Medium-Large: H (5.00mm) hook or size to obtain gauge. 3 1/4" Square.

Ch 4, join with a sl st to form a ring.

Rnd 1: With main color ch 3 (to count as dc). In ring make 2 dc, ch 2; (3 dc, ch 2) 3 times. Join with a sl st to top of first ch 3. Fasten off.

Rnd 2: Join contrasting color in any ch 2 sp. Ch 3. 2 dc, ch 2, 3 dc in same sp (corner made). * 3 dc, ch 2, 3 dc in next ch 2 sp, rep from * 2 times more. Join with a sl st to top of first ch 3. Fasten off.

Rnd 3: Join main color in any ch 2 sp. Ch 3. 2 dc, ch 2, 3 dc in same sp (corner made). 3 dc in next sp. *3 dc, ch 2, 3 dc in next ch 2 sp (corner made), 3 dc in next sp, rep from * 2 more times. Join with a sl st to top of first ch 3. Fasten off.

Join 5 squares together for each slipper (see photo). Join the row of 3 squares together to form a circle.

Toe Section

Ch 4, join with a sl st to form a ring.

Rnd 1: Ch 3. 11 dc in ring. Join with a sl st to top of first ch 3.

Rnd 2: Ch 3. 1 dc in same sp as last sl st. * 2 dc in next st, rep from * around. Join with a sl st to top of first ch 3. 24 dc.

Rnd 3: *For small size only.* Ch 3. 1 dc in same sp as last sl st. 1 dc in each of next 7 sts. *2 dc in next st. 1 dc in each of next 7 sts. Rep from * around. Join with a sl st to top of first ch 3. 27 dc.

Rnd 3: *For sizes medium and large.* Ch 3. 1 dc in same sp as last sl st. 1 dc in each of next 3 sts. *2 dc in next st. 1 dc in each of next 3 sts. Rep from * around. Join with a sl st to top of first ch 3. 30 dc.

Sew toe section to the circle of granny squares (see photo below).

Back Section

Note: You will now be working in rows for all sizes. Medium and Large instructions are in parenthesis.

With right side facing you attach yarn to the ch 2 sp of the first granny square (see photo below).

Row 1: Ch 3 (counts as 1st dc). Work 20 (22, 22) dc evenly across the two granny squares. 21 (23, 23) dc. Ch 3. Turn.

Row 2: *For medium and large sizes only.* Work even across row. 23 dc. Ch 3. Turn.

Row 3: *For large size only.* Work even across row. 23 dc. Ch 3. Turn.

Last row for all sizes: Dc in 9 (10, 10) sts. Work next 3 sts together as follows: (yo, insert hook in next st, draw up lp, yo, draw through 2 lps) 3 times, yo, draw through 4 lps on hook. 1 dc in each of next 9 (10, 10) sts. Fasten off leaving a length of yarn to sew center back of slipper.

With yarn end threaded in tapestry needle sew slipper heel together.

Ballet Flats

Instructions

Size: Small (5-6) Medium (7-8) Large (9-10)

Materials: Lily's Sugar'n Cream or any number 4 cotton yarn.

2.5 ounces (70.9g)

Tapestry or yarn needle

Hook: Size H (5.0mm) crochet hook or size to obtain gauge

Gauge: 4 dc = 1 inch 2 rows = 1 inch

Note: Numbers in parenthesis are for medium and large sizes.

Ch 4, join with a sl st to form a ring.

Rnd 1: Ch 3. 11 dc in ring. Join with a sl st to top of first ch 3.

Rnd 2: Ch 3. 1 dc in same sp as last sl st. * 2 dc in next st, rep from * around. Join with a sl st to top of first ch 3. 24 dc.

Rnd 3: For Small size only. Ch 3. 1 dc in same sp as last sl st. 1 dc in each of next 3 sts. *2 dc in next st. 1 dc in each of next 3 sts. Rep from * around. Join with a sl st to top of first ch 3. 30 dc.

Rnds 4-6: For small size only. Ch 3. 1 dc in each st around. Join with a sl st to top of first ch 3. 30 dc.

Rnd 3: For sizes medium and large. Ch 3. 1 dc in same sp as last sl st. 1 dc in each of next 5 sts. *2 dc in next st. 1 dc in each of next 5 sts. Rep from * around. Join with a sl st to top of first ch 3. 28 dc.

Rnd 4: For sizes medium and large. Ch 3. 1 dc in same sp as last sl st. 1 dc in each of next 6 sts. *2 dc in next st. 1 dc in each of next 6 sts. Rep from * around. Join with a sl st to top of first ch 3. 32 dc.

Rnds 5-7: For sizes medium and large. Ch 3. 1 dc in each st around. Join with a sl st to top of first ch 3. 32 dc.

Note: You will now be working in rows for all sizes. Medium and large instructions are in parenthesis.

Row 1: Ch 3. 1 dc in each of next 22 (24, 24) sts. Ch 3. Turn. 23 (25, 25) dc.

Rows 2-9 (10, 12): 1 dc in each st across. Ch 3. Turn. 23 (25, 25) dc.

Row 10 (11, 13): 1 dc in each of next 9 (10, 10) sts. Work next 3 sts together as follows: (yo, insert hook in next st, draw up lp, yo, draw through 2 lps) 3 times, yo, draw through 4 lps on hook. 1 dc in each of next 10 (11, 11) sts. Fasten off leaving a length of yarn to sew center back of slipper. With yarn end threaded in tapestry needle sew slipper heel together.

Edging

Rnd 1: Rejoin yarn with sc around bar of dc just to the left of heel. Sc around same bar. 2 sc around each bar and 1 sc in each st across toe. Join with a sl st to first sc. Fasten off.

Drawstring: Ch 85. Fasten off. Starting at heel weave through the top edge of slipper just under edging and through the dc's across the toe. See the photo below. Tie in a bow at center back.

Flowers: Make one large flower, one small flower, and one set of leaves for each slipper. Sew just off center of each slipper. Refer to photo of slipper for placement of flowers.

Instructions

Size: Approximately 2 inches for large flower and 1 inch for small flower.

Materials: Lily's Sugar'n Cream or any number 4 cotton yarn.

Small amounts in colors of your choice.

Tapestry or yarn needle

Hook: Size H (5.0mm) crochet hook

Note: Leave a 6 inch tail at beginning and end of the flowers and leaves to attach to project.

Large Flower: Ch 4. Join with a sl st to form a ring. Ch 3. 2 dc in ring, ch 3, sl st in ring. *Ch 3, 2 dc in ring, sl st in ring. Rep from * 3 more times. You will have 5 flower petals. Fasten off leaving a 6 inch tail of yarn.

Small Flower: Ch 7. 3 sc in 2nd ch from hook. 3 sc in each ch. Fasten off leaving a 6 inch tail of yarn. Coil flower and take a stitch or two to secure with tapestry needle and tail of yarn.

Leaves: Ch 4. Join with a sl st to form a ring. *Ch 10, sl st in ring. Rep from * 2 more times. You will have 3 leaves.

Assembly and attaching flowers: To assemble the large flowers place the small flower on top of large flower and with a tapestry needle draw tails of yarn from the small flower down through the large flower on either side of the center ring. Turn the large flower over and tie ends with an over hand knot. Trim ends of yarn close to the knot.

To attach large flower to a project take the ends of the large flower and with a tapestry needle take yarn ends down through the project on either side of a stitch. Tie ends with an over hand knot. Trim ends of yarn close to the knot. The leaves are attached the same way as the large flower.

Conclusion

I hope you enjoyed the patterns. Please consider leaving me a review. I value your opinion and would love to hear from you.

You can also visit my facebook fan page to leave a message or comment.

http://www.facebook.com/VickiBeckerAuthor

Visit my author page at Amazon for a list of my other needlework titles!

http://www.amazon.com/-/e/B009ZWK7Q6

Visit my web site for more needlework tips and free patterns!

http://vickisdesigns.com

You can email me

vicki@vickisdesigns.com

7967695R00015

Printed in Great Britain
by Amazon.co.uk, Ltd.,
Marston Gate.